Beautiful Washington

BEAUTIFUL WEST PUBLISHING COMPANY

CURRENT BOOKS
Alaska
California
Colorado
Hawaii
Montana
Mt. Hood
Northern California
Oregon
Utah
Washington
Western Impressions

FORTHCOMING BOOKS
Arizona
California Missions
Georgia
Lewis & Clark Country
Maryland
Mexico
New Mexico
New York
Oregon Coast
San Francisco
Sierra Nevada
Southern California
Virginia

OTHER ITEMS
25 Oregon Weekend Adventures
Photographic Prints & Placemats

Send for complete catalog, 50¢

Beautiful West Publishing Company
202 N.W. 21st Avenue ● Portland, Oregon, 97209

Beautiful Washington

Featuring RAY ATKESON Photography

Text by Paul M. Lewis

Third Printing September 1977

Published by Beautiful West Publishing Company
202 N.W. 21st Avenue, Portland, Oregon 97209
Robert D. Shangle, Publisher

ISBN Number 0-915796-02-3 (Paperback)
ISBN Number 0-915796-05-8 (Hard Bound)

Copyright © 1974 by Beautiful West Publishing Company
Printed in the United States of America

RAY ATKESON

Ray Atkeson has photographed Washington and the Pacific Northwest for more than thirty years. He was born in the Midwest and spent his early years in Illinois and Missouri. So the Northwest is all the more exciting to him for the comparisons he is able to draw with other areas.

When he moved to the Northwest he became a photographer for a commercial studio in Portland. On weekends he roamed the Northwest with his camera. His early work was purchased by national publications and newspapers such as The New York Times, The Kansas City Star, The Houston Chronicle, and The London Times.

Since 1946 his work has appeared frequently in Holiday, Time, Sports Illustrated, National Geographic, and many other publications of national and international reputation.

His enthusiasm for mountaineering and the outdoors adds the extra dimension that raises his portraits of nature to the highest level of interpretative art.

CONTENTS

Introduction 7

Puget Sound 10

Olympic Peninsula 14

The Coast 18

Southern Washington 22

The Mountains 58

Central Washington 62

Eastern Washington 66

Map 70

Wild Flowers of Washington 71

CREDITS

Photography by Ray Atkeson
Lithography by Fremont Litho, Inc., Fremont, California

Beautiful Washington

TUCKED away in the northwest corner of the continental United States is a smallish state by western standards. In terms of land area, it doesn't quite measure up to Oregon on the south, and Idaho and Montana to the east, states that, along with Washington, make up the Northwest.

Washingtonians—natives, residents, and temporary transplants from other places—are fond of starting with the above premise when launching into an (admittedly prejudiced) analysis of the unique virtues of the state of Washington. They let you absorb that modest preamble, then hit you with a triumphant haymaker: within the state's borders is more scenic variety than in any other state, Hawaii and Alaska not excepted. Huddled as it is in its corner with two other states—Oregon and Idaho—to which "beautiful" is an understatement, Washington's brag could seem more like a challenge than a reality. When you consider the western United States, with its myriad natural wonders scattered through California, Nevada, Utah, Arizona, New Mexico, Colorado, and so on, the boast may sound a little questionable. But only if you don't know Washington. "Insiders" are aware that their corner of the country has a sample of just about every natural attribute found in various parts of the rest of the country.

For those who have been in the dark about this not inconsiderable piece of knowledge, this book will be a colorful revelation about a colorful state. For the initiates, inside and outside of Washington's borders, there are page after page of sumptuous examples of Ray Atkeson color photography. Perhaps they will even be surprised to see some familiar landmark presented in a pose not quite as they remembered it, metamorphosed by the creative eye of the photographer. All the landscapes, with their brilliant hues and subtle, subdued ones, do show handily that the word "contrast" is understating the case for Washington. You will see every kind of scenery. Take the coast: on the south are long, low, sandy beaches; to the north, on the Olympic Peninsula, massive cliffs and headlands cut through the beaches and the near shore is laced with free-standing rocks and pinnacles. Take the Olympic Peninsula: in an area about 70 miles from east to west and the same north to south are violent variations in climate and topography, including the mighty mass of the Olympic Mountains, with their close-knit circle of glaciated peaks; on the west side of the peninsula are the famous rain forests of the Olympic National Park, one of the wettest spots on earth; in the lee of the Olympics, on the peninsula's north coast, is a mild climatic band about 20 miles wide where rainfall averages only 14 inches annually. Take the Cascades themselves, a high north-south range whose volcanic spires tower in awe-inspiring majesty.

Consider Puget Sound, unique blending of landscape and seascape, whose almost infinite patterns and relationships are a never-ending delight to the marine explorer. Consider also, on the east slope of the Cascades, the rich agricultural Wenatchee and Yakima valleys, paradise for farmers and orchardists. On the north, in the Okanogan Highlands, are the "Texas-style" cattle ranches and old mining towns, relics of the last century's hunt for gold. To the south, the Columbia Basin is made productive by the tremendous dams of the Reclamation Project.

In the southeast corner the landscape takes on yet another character, for here are fertile valleys, semi-desert lands, barren mountains, canyons, coulees, and deep gorges cut by such celebrated rivers as the Snake and the Palouse.

Some like it hot, some like it cold—or in between. Some like it damp, others, dry. Some like to live high up. Others take to the valleys. Washington has all these climates and landscapes and the bewildering variety of plant and animal life that is at home in these environments.

This modest-sized state has so much of everything that it looms larger than life. There are even some features in the "biggest" category: Long Beach on the south coast, 28 miles of the longest driveable beach in the world; Mt. Rainier, biggest in bulk and tallest of any separate peak in the continental United States; Seattle, biggest Northwest city; Olympic Peninsula, most extensive rain forest.

In these times when we are beginning to become self-conscious about our place in nature and about our responsibilities in the way we interact with it, Washingtonians, like other Americans who live in the midst of spectacular natural beauty, are rising to the challenge of their role as trustees of their environment. The State of Washington is making certain that the riches it has been given will be returned with interest to succeeding generations.

(Right) MT. ST. HELENS ... Mt. St. Helens, "The Fujiyama of America" towers above Spirit Lake which is nestled in the vast evergreen forests of Washington's Cascade Range.

Puget Sound

ALL of us have, at one time or another, imagined we were in a far-off land, perhaps living on a tiny island in a calm sea dotted with other islands close enough to be friendly but not close enough to be nosy. Some of the islands are entirely covered with thick evergreen forests, while others front the water with steep cliffs, secret coves, or low, sandy beaches. All around the horizon is spectacular scenery, mostly mountain ranges raising glaciated spires to the sky. At night, in our imaginings, we see several glowing points on the horizon that must be cities—one of the light areas, to the south, is especially impressive. We're glad our island world can be so remote from, while yet so near to, those crowded-together people places.

Too bad we're dreaming, we might say in our dream. But to anyone who has ever been to Puget Sound, especially in the north Sound where the San Juans lie, this is real. Fortunately, Puget Sound really exists, improbable as that may seem. This inland sea with its hundreds of islands, multitudes of waterways, harbors, coves, inlets, and shores, has a miraculous beauty that is all the more amazing for its being next door to the most densely populated area in the Northwest, the Seattle-Tacoma metropolitan complex. In fact, the major proportion of Washington State's population is encamped on the shores of the Sound. Nearly all of the biggest cities have their feet in its waters—for instance, Olympia, Tacoma, Seattle, Bremerton, Everett, and Bellingham.

A map of the Sound can only give an approximation of the complicated interlacings of land and waterways that make up this unique part of the world. The Kitsap Peninsula, itself saved from island status only by a narrow neck of land near its base, bulges importantly over much of the lower Sound. Hood Canal slices between it and the Olympic Peninsula on the west, and the Sound proper separates it from the east shore. Kitsap has a wealth of fishing ports and natural attractions related to its land-sea ambiance. Its major city is Bremerton, of Navy Yard fame.

The Puget Sound's "highways" are the ferry routes with their fleets of auto-carrying ferries that sail the inland seas between the cities of the east shore—Seattle, Tacoma, Everett, and the Kitsap and Olympic peninsulas, thirteen islands, and Vancouver Island. Ferry travel through these waters with their variety of landscapes and harbors is a rich experience indeed.

The ferry rides are sufficient unto themselves even with no car along to take you somewhere at the end of the voyage.

The best-known chunks of real estate here are the San Juan Islands. Strictly speaking, they aren't even in the Sound, which officially includes only the southern portion, beginning with the entrance to Hood Canal. But the San Juans are popularly considered to be part of it. They number 172 big and little islands and are scattered all over the northern arm of the inland sea. Ferries carry people and things to some of these islands. The best-known trip by ferry is the one between Anacortes, Washington, and Sidney, B.C. The three-hour route slips through the islands and visits some of the small ports on Lopez, Shaw, Orcas, and San Juan islands. Private boats or charter boats are, of course, other means of transportation around the San Juans. One of the fascinations of the islands is their impression of remoteness, even though they're not remote in the matter of distance. Many of them are uninhabited and some are for sale.

The thorough exploration of the San Juans would require more than a lifetime of looking by a dedicated mariner. But that does not deter the weekend sailor, who can usually find a snug, secluded harbor to suit his fancy, wherever in the islands his wanderlust leads him. There is no commercial development of any consequence, although resorts are plentiful. The facilities offered are of the modest, cottage type. A popular summer evening pastime is the beach picnic, with driftwood fires, clam bakes, and fish suppers.

The biggest of the San Juans is Orcas Island. It has a comfortable, resort atmosphere, with settlements around the island connected by paved roads. For the tourist there are campsites, boating, swimming, and fishing in Moran State Park. The highest point in the San Juans is on Orcas (Mt. Constitution—2,409 feet), from where there is a full-circle view of the other islands.

San Juan Island is the most populated. Its city, Friday Harbor, is also the county seat of San Juan County, which includes most of the San Juan group. This island once had its troubles with the Indians, and some of the blockhouses built during this time are still standing. Its most memorable moment in history came in 1859 when it was the site of the "pig war," a comic-opera dispute between the Americans and the British over who owned the island. It began

PUGET SOUND

when an American settler shot a pig that belonged to an Englishman, riling the (British) authorities. The American called for help, and both Americans and British landed troops (100 each, by agreement). In the years that followed, the garrisons whiled away the idle time by throwing parties and giving banquets for each other until in 1872 the German emperor, as arbitrator, awarded the San Juan Islands to the United States.

Puget Sound is also a big lumber country—off the water, of course. The ample rainfall makes the Douglas Fir grow 200 feet tall and four to six feet in diameter. While the loggers don't actually drop the trees from the banks to the water, the accessibility of the inland sea makes transportation a relatively simple affair. Hood Canal is a busy waterway for the transport of logs from the forests of the Olympic Peninsula. They are formed into rafts which are taken in tow by tugs. Brands, similar to cattle brands, are used to identify logs in case a raft breaks up.

The complicated land-sea interplay that is Puget Sound may some day be changed by slow-working natural forces into something that has little resemblance to the Sound of today. That will probably not happen before thousands, or even hundreds of thousands of years. One natural force that can radically and quickly alter the nature of this fantastic fairyland of island-strewn inland waterways is man. The power of the human race to manipulate its surroundings in a cavalier fashion is especially dangerous in an environment whose complicated interrelationships require special handling. We should remain aware of this when we consider how we can "improve" and "develop" areas whose charm and unique character make them especially popular. We can only hope that Puget Sound will never suffer such depredation at the hands of its human inhabitants.

(Following Page) SWIFT RESERVOIR ... Tall, stately fir trees and autumn-tinted vine maple fringe the shoreline of Swift Reservoir, created by a dam on the Lewis River in southern Washington.

(Upper Left) WASHINGTON COAST ... Longbeach, Washington, the longest driveable beach in the world, (you can drive your car for 28 miles on it) stretches up the Washington coastline from North Head Lighthouse in the foreground.

(Upper Right) WASHINGTON COAST ... Melting fog hovers over the rock-studded shoreline at Point Grenville on the Washington Coast.

(Lower) BIRD CREEK MEADOWS ... A clear stream flows down through a flower-sprinkled alpine meadow in Bird Creek Meadows near timberline on Mt. Adams in southern Washington. The area is popular with campers, picnickers, hikers, and botanists.

Olympic Peninsula

THE Olympic Peninsula is such a variety of things it's quite impossible to characterize briefly. To make things easier, the Olympic coastal strip has been discussed in the chapter dealing with the state's coastline. The obvious preliminary things to say about this land mass concern its size and shape. On the map its squarish contour looks something like a thumb or big toe appended to the body of the country. Distances are moderate: the peninsula is about 75 miles east-to-west at its widest point and the same from the northern tip to Grays Harbor at its base. It is bordered on the east by Hood Canal, on the north by the Strait of Juan de Fuca, and on the west by the Pacific Ocean.

U.S. Highway 101 makes a neat loop around the peninsula, following the coast along the eastern side and as far as Port Angeles on the north. But then, as if distracted by its proximity to the superlative Olympic Mountains, it heads inland and for a time skirts the national park containing these craggy peaks. Although avoiding the coast for most of the rest of its circuit, it stays close enough to the perimeter to enclose most of the peninsula's variety.

The road takes off from Olympia, Washington's capital, and begins its meandering route along the wooded shore of Hood Canal. Along the 30 miles of the canal are fishing resorts and gravel beaches popular with clam diggers (when the weather is right). Spur roads in this stretch lead up steep river valleys of the Hamma Hamma, Duckabush, and Dosewallips flowing down from the Olympic mountains.

At the northeastern corner of the peninsula is Discovery Bay, named in 1792 by the English sea captain George Vancouver after his ship. Following a side road on the Bay's eastern shore we come to Port Townsend, on the extreme northeast tip of a finger of land edged by the bay and Puget Sound. Port Townsend has distinction as a kind of architectural museum where the Victorian buildings have been preserved and restored. The town has been "frozen" to look about the way it did in the last century, when it was the most important entrance to the Sound.

Farther west is Port Angeles, the peninsula's largest town, and lumber center for the north peninsula. Its excellent natural harbor, protected on the west by a narrow slice of land, accommodates ocean freighters, mostly for loading with export logs. Port Angeles is also the main northern entrance to Olympic National Park. From here Hurricane Ridge highway takes a scenic course for 13 miles up to Hurricane Ridge Lodge on Big Meadow. At the lodge the closeup panorama of the Olympics is a show-stopper, and a tourist-stopper. Lordly Mt. Olympus is center stage, standing above the jumbled mass of the peaks on its flanks. The ridge road goes through dense forests along the way to Big Meadow and Obstruction Point farther along. Occasional viewpoints allow the traveler to look down on Port Angeles, northeast to the San Juan Islands and Mt. Baker, and, on the very top of the ridge, to take in the whole inner Olympics.

Olympic National Park was dedicated as a wilderness in 1946, which means that it has remained in its natural state. West of Port Angeles, U.S. 101 brushes its northern edge briefly, but no roads cross the mountains, although some spur roads go up the valleys. But it is one of the easiest wildernesses to penetrate and enjoy, if one is willing to do it on foot. The park has at least three distinct regions: the north, west, and east. The north contains some of the best woodland, the biggest lake (Lake Crescent), spectacular alpine meadows, and the heaviest snowfall.

The west, or "wet" side, including the coastal strip, receives up to 150 inches of rain annually from clouds that pile up against the mountains, after having been driven in on prevailing southwest Pacific winds. Here is where the trees grow to colossal size in a rain forest that is unique on the face of the earth. Everything is mantled in moss and the undergrowth is extremely dense. Rain forests don't grow different species of plants from other forests—every growing thing just does it more exuberantly and in a bigger way. Open spaces on the forest floor are kept so in part by the browsing of the famed Olympic elk. But even in this dense, jungle-like environment, the forest is far from gloomy. A soft, green light filters through and is reflected by the leaves and mosses. The Bogachiel and Hoh River valleys contain some of the best examples of rain forest, and trails through these forests are very popular with hikers.

The southeast side of the wilderness is the "dry" part, in comparison with the rain forest. This area is notable for its dense forests of fir, cedar, and hemlock, and for its steep, narrow river valleys.

Once the highway has curved around the Olympic

OLYMPIC PENINSULA

National Park it has nearly finished its odyssey on the peninsula. Before bending sharply inland and shooting straight south for Hoquiam-Aberdeen at the peninsula's base, the road cuts through 11 miles of the park's coastal strip.

On the north coast are some places of interest looking out on the Strait of Juan de Fuca. West along the coast from Port Angeles State Highway 112 sometimes rides high over the strait, sometimes stays level with the beach. Along the way to the northwest tip of the peninsula it passes tree farms, fishing villages, and lumber towns. Sekiu, near Neah Bay, is home to a whole fleet of boats that crowd its bay when the salmon are migrating from ocean to river. Here, big log rafts are made up in a technique called "booming" and towed by tug to mills. Neah Bay, at the end of the highway, is an Indian fishing town and has been engaged in this activity since long before the white man's arrival. Commercial fishing fleets are active in the summer here, but disappear in the winter, when Neah Bay is buffeted by the stormy ocean. Cape Flattery, at the very tip, is at the end of a six-mile road from Neah Bay plus a one-mile hike. From the high ground of the cape there's a splendid view of the pounding ocean and of solitary Tatoosh Island with its lighthouse.

An excursion into the wilds of the Olympics or around other parts of the Olympic Peninsula leaves the traveler with a sense of wonder and gratitude. Wonder at the lavish hand of nature in fashioning so much beauty. Gratitude that we seem to be learning our responsibilities in caring for such beauty.

(Following Two Pages) COLUMBIA RIVER GORGE ... The Columbia River Gorge is shown where the mighty river flows through the Cascade Range between Washington and Oregon. The photo was taken from Cape Horn on Washington's Evergreen Highway, U.S. No. 197.

The Coast

WASHINGTON'S face to the Pacific is at least two-faced. More accurately, many-faced. The coastline is about two-thirds Olympic Peninsula coast and one-third Washington's south coast, if we consider just the shoreline that fronts the Pacific Ocean. But Washington is never that simple, and emphatically not in the matter of coastlines. The northern segment, or what is called the Olympic seashore, goes from one point to another without a great many detours. It is measureable by counting the miles —about 100—from Cape Flattery to the North Bay of Grays Harbor. But along the lower coast the Pacific has in effect taken two big swallows of shoreline and created Grays Harbor and Willapa Bay—the Twin Harbors, as they are called. If we add to the coastal mileage the enormous stretches of shoreline contained in these two extensive inlets, the mileage is about equal to the northern, or Olympic, part.

South of Cape Flattery at the northern end is Point of Arches, one of the most beautiful parts of the entire coast. Rocks and rock islets are scattered in profusion offshore, many having been tunneled through by the incessant crashing of the waves (see page 18). Tidepools and arches can be reached at low tide. Cape Alava, a few miles south, is the westernmost point in the three Pacific Coast states. At high tide it beats out Cape Flattery for that honor by a few hundred feet. At low tide it gives up the title to a small island linked to the mainland by a sandspit. The island, named Indian, or Cannonball Island, has "cannonball" rocks whose spherical shape has not been completely explained by scientists. Cape Alava is the recipient, even more than other coastal "catch basins," of an enormous amount of lumber and other materials cast up by the sea.

Cape Alava, like many parts of this coast, has no roads leading to it. It is reached by four miles of trails from the end of the road at Ozette. The cape is also at the northern end of the Olympic National Park's coastal strip, where dense forests and steep headlands south to Rialto Beach (17 miles) make hiking a reasonable venture only for the experienced and well-prepared. At Rialto Beach and La Push the beach is reached by a road. La Push, on the Quillayute Indian Reservation, is a fishing village which caters to tourists, renting charter boats for salmon fishing and offering Indian articles for sale. The wilderness beach itself is flat and easily traveled on foot, except for the headlands encountered now and then. But beach hikers need to have a wary knowledge of high and low tides and to be on the watch for severe weather conditions.

Toleak Point, six miles south of La Push, is easily reached by hikers and is popular as a wilderness site. Three headlands are encountered along the way, but two of them can be skirted at low tide. At high tide they must be climbed. Trails are well marked, and the scenery is as varied as it is on the beach. Toleak Point is a sanctuary for bald eagles, one of the few places outside of Alaska where these majestic birds thrive.

Down the coast through the Olympic strip are the Hoh River and the Hoh Indian Reservation. Not much can be said about this spot in human terms, but the Hoh River valley is a magnificent example of rain forest. Ruby Beach, a little way to the south, is the northern point where Highway 101 reaches out to the coast of the Olympic Peninsula and hugs it for 11 miles, the only part of the coast that is visited by this "Olympic loop" road. This strip is usually explored in short hikes from automobile starting points on the highway. In spite of the presence of the road, there are few signs of civilization. Offshore pinnacles and stacks, and tideland wilderness are the same as they were when no white man had seen them. Queets, at the southern end of the shoreside stretch of road, is an Indian village on the northern edge of the Quinault Indian Reservation. Access to the reservation is regulated by the Indians, as are all hunting and fishing. The Quinault region is best for seeing the rain forest by car, because U.S. 101 goes through it. There are plenty of trails for those who still prefer more intimate exploration.

Past the Quinault area is a series of small communities that qualify as beach resorts. After the wilderness coast the scene has changed to the more familiar, "managed" beaches, beautiful, flat, sandy stretches with tourist facilities. Clamming is popular here and is excellent all the way down to Grays Harbor. The south coast, with its twins, Grays and Willapa, is the land of summer resorts. Both harbors are guarded by narrow fingers of land. North Beach Peninsula's 28 miles of sand beach forms the skinny arm of Willapa Bay. More familiarly called Long Beach, this knife-blade sand spit has long been a popular vacation area for Portlanders, who came to Ilwaco by steamboat during the nineties, taking a narrow-gauge

THE COAST

railroad to reach the resort towns strung along the beach. It is claimed that even in winter the peninsula's long beaches are inviting. A road now connects the towns of the peninsula, but no through road reaches this long sand spit. One of Washington's oldest towns—Oysterville—is here. It has some buildings dating from the 1860s.

Willapa Bay is home to a lot of oysters, raised on private oyster farms. Grayland, midway between the harbors, has long been a cranberry growing center, from the time some early Finnish growers established the first bogs. The state highways that explore the middle coast include Grays Harbor in their routes: 109 follows the north shore and 105 goes along the south harbor, reaching over to Willapa Bay's north shore. So the Twin Harbors are easy to explore by car, especially since U.S. 101 roams the east and south shores of Willapa.

A summary tour of Washington's inimitable coastal variety can give only an incomplete idea about it. A look at the pictorial evidence in this chapter will probably do more to stir the appreciative faculty. For example, Ruby Beach, with its driftwood and offshore pinnacles, on page 18; Cape Flattery and Tatoosh Island, on page 16, the long, flat, driveable sand of Long Beach (North Beach Peninsula), on page 15. The sample of the coast depicted here in pictures and text may serve as a reminder that man is really just a minor part of other aspects of nature. His most important goal on this planet may be to learn to live in harmony with nature's complex design, of which the Washington coast is an example.

(Upper Right) NORTH HEAD LIGHTHOUSE ... This lighthouse stands defiantly on a headland overlooking the mouth of the Columbia River and many miles of southern Washington coastline. Many ships have found their graveyard on rocks or sand spits within sight of North Head.

(Upper Left) TATOOSH ISLAND ... Tatoosh Island stands guard at the entrance to the Strait of Juan de Fuca just off Cape Flattery on the northwest tip of Washington's Olympic Peninsula. Coast Guard facilities operate from Tatoosh.

(Lower) WASHINGTON COAST ... Pacific Surf rolls in past rocky pinnacles to break on the black sands of Ruby Beach in Olympic National Park.

Southern Washington

IF THERE really is a southern Washington it must be that part of the state along the Columbia, the part whose rivers and streams drain directly into that immense trough. For convenience we have so designated this general region, because to stray very far north at any point along the riverine country is to identify with another part of the state.

The town of Ilwaco is just inside the rough waters of the mouth of the Columbia. If one drives the 200 miles from Ilwaco to Horse Heaven Hills the pace is much slower than on the Oregon side, where a super-duper highway zips the motorist past all that sumptuous scenery before he has had time to look at it. The headlands at the mouth are rugged and forested, but excellent viewpoints to watch freighters getting tossed around while crossing the Columbia River bar. This stormy meeting of the waters has brought to grief hundreds of ships, some of whose remains can still be seen sinking into the sand of North Beach Peninsula (Long Beach).

Upriver from Ilwaco is Megler, where ferries crossed to Astoria, Oregon, before the Astoria-Megler toll bridge was built a few years ago. This stretch of river is lined with some pleasant, quiet villages. At Cathlamet is a bridge to Puget Island, worth a visit for its gentle, pastoral scenery and small-boat moorings. The cities of Longview and Kelso, at the point of the river where it turns south toward Portland, are busy wood processing centers. The giant Weyerhaeuser company has its headquarters near here. At this point Interstate 5 becomes the road along the river, but alternate routes are available for those who are repelled by the robotic rhythm of the multiple-lane freeway. At Longview there is a mile-and-a-half-long cantilever bridge that reaches over to Rainier, Oregon. At this point on the river the spectacularly beautiful and symmetrical Mt. St. Helens appears center stage, due east. Rugged Mt. Adams, farther east, is also part of the view.

Vancouver is across from Portland, Oregon's first city. Vancouver is the first city among Washington's Columbia River towns. Another distinction: it is the oldest city in the state. Fort Vancouver was founded in 1824 by the Hudson's Bay Company. Here the Columbia takes a straight easterly direction. Not far beyond Vancouver the river has fashioned a showy setting on its north bank. Beacon Rock rises a sheer 850 feet above the river east of Washougal, but is easily climbed for a magnificent view of the Columbia Gorge because of the well-engineered trail worked into its sides. The outlook to the east shows the river enfolded between its high, forested banks, with Mt. Hood in Oregon and Mt. Adams to the north posing in the wings. To the west, the Columbia River islands stand out, as do the cliffs of the Oregon side of the gorge.

The next important sight upriver is Bonneville Dam, last downstream dam and first to be built on the river. This part of southern Washington encompasses the Gifford Pinchot National Forest, which includes the aforementioned St. Helens and Adams. A bit past the town of Stevenson, the Wind River comes tumbling out of this forest. Its course is followed for 15 miles by a paved road. A trip up this spectacular canyon brings multiple rewards, one of which is crossing the Wind River on a suspension bridge 250 feet over the stream. Another is the sight, to the north, of Mt. St. Helens, when the observer gets high up enough to look across the long stretch of forest.

Although it's rather a comedown, a few miles east on the Columbia highway, the crest of the Cascades is crossed. Now the forest changes from fir to pine, is less dense, and the landscape is browner. This is also apple and huckleberry country. From the town of White Salmon, State Highway 141 heads for the recreation area around Mt. Adams. The area around the mountain was left quite open by long ago forest blazes. The 12,300-foot peak has nine separate glaciers and many ice caves. One of these is near Troutlake and readily accessible. From roads that go up Mt. Adams to timberline, the hiker can easily reach the snow level and get marvelous views of St. Helens and Hood, or even of the crest of Adams itself. But it's still a long, hard climb for experienced mountaineers to get to that crest.

Mt. St. Helens, anchoring the western edge of the Pinchot forest, is one of the most beautiful peaks of Washington's Cascades. Its base is approachable by car. Spirit Lake, 2½ miles long, lies at the north base, at an elevation of 3,200 feet. The lake is surrounded by forested cliffs except to the south, where it opens to the snow-topped peak. The lake and the mountain, together with the back country, make up a rich recreation area.

Moving up the Columbia again, we reach The

(Preceding Page) CAPE FLATTERY ... A tree-fringed rock pinnacle stands guard at the mouth of a surf-scoured cove which frames a vista the lighthouse on famed Tatoosh Island, a half mile offshore from rugged Cape Flattery. Winter storms lash the coves and caves at the foot the cape, creating an entirely different picture from this tranquil low tide scene.

SOUTHERN WASHINGTON

Dalles Dam, which holds back the Columbia to form Lake Celilo extending 24 miles to John Day Dam. John Day, the newest dam (completed in 1968) on the lower Columbia, backs the river up 76 miles to McNary Dam, which stretches between Benton County, Washington, and Umatilla County, Oregon. Lake Umatilla, thus created, is second only in size to Roosevelt Lake on the upper Columbia. These dams and others on the river are giant power producers and bring water to otherwise arid regions. Klickitat County, stretching along the river from the east slope of the Cascades for about 70 miles, and southern Benton County next to the east, have developed enormously as agricultural marketplaces since these dams were constructed on the lower Columbia.

As it has for eons, the mighty Columbia exerts a mighty control over the destiny of what is now southern Washington. Before civilized man came, the inhabitants simply marveled at the immense power of the river to shape the land as it pleased. Now man has learned to leash and manipulate for his benefit this priceless natural resource.

(Upper) GRAYS RIVER COVERED BRIDGE ... This covered bridge spanning the Grays River in southwestern Washington is the only such bridge in use in the state. It was constructed in 1905.

(Lower) WASHINGTON STREAM ... A delightful little forest stream pours over mossy ledges and seeks its way around moss-covered stones in the Cascade Range of southern Washington.

(Upper Right) SKAMAKAWA ... The little fishing port of Skamakawa, Washington, is just off the Columbia River.
(Upper Left) MARYHILL MUSEUM ... The Maryhill Museum stands regally alone on the Columbia hills of southern Washington overlooking the Columbia River.
(Lower) KLICKITAT RIVER ... Autumn touches oak foliage with warm color along the shore and on hillsides beside the Klickitat River in southeastern Washington.

(Upper) WASHINGTON COAST ... Surf fishing is popular from the steep beaches along the northern coast of Washington. This is one of the beaches on the Olympic National Park coastal strip.

(Upper Right) WASHINGTON COAST ... Spectacular offshore rocks or "stacks" thrust high above the blue surf of the Pacific at Point of Arches on the remote coastline of Washington's Olympic Peninsula. Several holes or tunnels and caves created by pounding surf account for the name of this area that can be reached only by several miles of hiking or by small boat when the sea is calm.

(Lower) RUBY BEACH ... What a spot for beachcombing! Surf-scoured logs and driftwood are entwined in a fantastic demonstration of the power of the sea, which often lashes rocky pinnacles and stacks that stand defiantly despite the ravages of time.

(Upper Right) CAPE FLATTERY ... Rocky pinnacles and stacks stand defiantly above the surf at the foot of Cape Flattery, at the extreme northwest tip of the Olympic Peninsula. Numerous coves like this surround the Cape. Most of them are inaccessible. Pacific storms hurl angry surf high up into these coves.
(Upper Left) OLYMPIC RAIN FOREST ... Club moss drapes maple trees in Olympic National Park. The moss which sometimes reaches several feet below tree bows is self-sustaining. It gets nourishment from the moist atmosphere.
(Lower) OLYMPIC RAIN FOREST ... These grand old maple trees draped in a heavy blanket of moss bear witness to an annual precipitation of 150 to 200 inches in the famed Olympic Rain Forest, Olympic National Park.

(Upper) OLYMPIC RAIN FOREST ... Moss-draped maple and alder trees form a canopy over a small stream in the Quinault River Valley in Olympic National Park.

(Lower) OLYMPIC RAIN FOREST ... Autumn foliage has decorated a rain-soaked road which penetrates the heart of the famed Olympic Rain Forest in Olympic National Park.

(Upper Left) OLYMPIC MOUNTAINS ... Glacier-clad Mt. Olympus, highest in the Olympic Range, rises above the Hoh River Valley.
(Upper Right) OLYMPIC NATIONAL PARK ... A couple of deer feed contentedly on Hurricane Ridge in Olympic National Park.
(Lower) OLYMPIC RAIN FOREST ... A trail winds over a carpet of moss in the famed Olympic Rain Forest, Olympic National Park.
(Following Left Page) SAN JUAN ISLANDS ... A sunset ripples across the waters of Puget Sound on the eastern edge of the San Juan Islands.
(Following Right Page) NORTH CASCADES NATIONAL PARK ... From Cascades Pass, trails radiate to various points of interest and mountain climbing routes. Towering above are the Triplets, Cascade Peak, and Johannesburg Mountain.

(Preceding Two Pages) LAKE CRESCENT ... Leaves of an old maple tree, carpet the shoreline of Crescent Lake in Olympic National Park.
(Upper Left) CASCADE MOUNTAIN STREAM ... Clear water stream cascades down through a gorge in northern Washington's Cascades.
(Upper Right) BIG FOUR MOUNTAIN ... The massive crags of Big Four Mountain tower 4,000 feet above a meadow in the Cascade Range.
(Lower) GOAT ROCKS WILDERNESS ... An old timberline tree reaches skyward and sets off the slopes of Old Snowy, one of the highest mountains in the Goat Rocks Wilderness of the Cascades.

(Upper) BONANZA PEAK ... The lofty summit crags of Bonanza Peak and a cloud banner are reflected in a beautiful alpine pool near Lyman Lake in the Glacier Peak Wilderness.
(Lower) GLACIER PEAK WILDERNESS ... These beautiful alpine meadows are on Cloudy Pass in the Glacier Peak Wilderness of northern Washington's Cascades. The rugged crest of Fortress Mountain looms over a snow-patched rocky ridge.
(Following Two Pages) MT. RAINIER NATIONAL PARK ... Fluffy seed pods of western anemone, sometimes called Old Man of the Mountains, stand out in on the slopes of the Tatoosh Range as clouds gather about Mt. Rainier.

(Upper Right) MT. BAKER ... Mt. Baker towers in wintry splendor above the snowfields on Kulshan Ridge.

(Upper Left) GLACIER PEAK WILDERNESS ... Image Lake, Jewel of the North Cascade Range, nestles in a beautiful setting of alpine meadows on Miner's Ridge high above evergreen forests of the Suiattle River Valley. This is the heart of the vast Glacier Peak Wilderness and a popular area for hikers and campers.

(Lower) KACHESS LAKE ... Autumn sunshine gleams across the waters of Kachess Lake in a Cascades valley. Vine maple foilage shown here stages the most vivid show of color of all Northwest foliage.

(Lower) WENATCHEE RIVER ... Autumn has spread glorious color around the Wenatchee River where it rushes down the eastern slopes of the Cascades, through Tumwater Canyon.

(Upper) DRY FALLS STATE PARK ... The greatest waterfalls on earth once roared over these tremendous cliffs of Dry Falls State Park in eastern Washington, when the mighty Columbia River was forced down the Grand Coulee by glaciers.

(Upper Right) PALOUSE GRAIN FIELDS ... Late afternoon sunlight skims across the Palouse grain fields of eastern Washington, emphasizing all the undulations of the rolling hills. The photo was made from the crest of historic Steptoe Butte. Grain elevators in the town of Steptoe reach into the sunshine from a distant valley.

(Upper Left) STEPTOE BUTTE ... Historic Steptoe Butte towers above grainfields and flower-carpeted meadows of Eastern Washington's Palouse country.

(Lower) HERITAGE LAKE ... Autumn-tinted larch trees (often called tamaracks) weave a golden mosaic pattern among the pines above Heritage Lake, one of a chain of small lakes in northeastern Washington known as Little Pend Oreille Lakes.

(Upper Right) GRAND COULEE DAM ... Grand Coulee Dam, a mile long and 350 feet high, harnesses the mighty Columbia River in eastern Washington. From here, hydroelectric power and water pumped from Roosevelt Lake, behind the dam, reach out to industrial cities and to the vast Columbia Basin Reclamation Project.

(Upper Left) GRAND COULEE DAM ... A full moon shines in the eastern Washington sky above Grand Coulee dam as colored floodlights illuminate the giant spillway.

(Lower) GRANDE RONDE RIVER ... Delicate hues of autumn tint the shoreline and the steep hillsides above the Grande Ronde River in southeastern Washington. The Grande Ronde is born in northeastern Oregon but flows thru a section of southeastern Washington to its confluence with the Snake River.

(Preceding Two Pages) HOOD CANAL ... Rhododendron, the state flower of Washington, photographed on the Olympic Peninsula's Mt. Walker overlooking Hood Canal.
(Upper Left) PALOUSE FALLS STATE PARK ... The Palouse River plunges over a high lava cliff into the depths of Palouse Canyon.
(Upper Right) WASHINGTON HARVEST ... Modern combines make short work of a field of wheat in the Palouse region of eastern Washington.
(Lower) KLICKITAT RIVER ... The Klickitat River is a silver ribbon in the bronze and mauve colors of autumn in southeastern Washington.

(Upper Left) EASTERN WASHINGTON ... A snowbound ranch in southeastern Washington's Klickitat Valley.
(Upper Right) EASTERN WASHINGTON FARM ... Well-kept farm buildings contrast with wheat fields just sprouting a new crop in autumn.
(Lower) SPOKANE RIVER ... The beauty of forests and river are preserved for visitors to Riverside State Park which borders the Spokane River.
(Following Page) MT. RAINIER ... Stately evergreens line the shoreline of Lake Eunice in Mt. Rainier National Park. The 14,410-foot, glacier-clad dome towers above the lake.

(Upper Left) GLACIER PEAK WILDERNESS, WASHINGTON ... Rugged peaks of Washington's North Cascade Range reach high into the blue sky above flower-carpeted alpine meadows at Buck Creek Pass in the Glacier Peak Wilderness.
(Upper Right) WASHINGTON PASS ... Spires and cliffs of Silver Star Mountain tower high above the North Cascades Highway.
(Lower) IMAGE LAKE ... Image Lake reflects Glacier Peak. The lake is in the Glacier Peak Wilderness area of the North Cascade Range.
(Following Two Pages) WASHINGTON GRAINFIELDS ...Pine trees on Kamiak Butte State Park frame a vista of grainfields near Pullman.

(Upper Right) SAN JUAN ISLANDS ... A Washington state ferry glides through the heart of the San Juan Islands en route from Anacortes to Sidney on Vancouver Island.

(Lower Left) PUGET SOUND ... A seagoing cargo ship headed for Seattle passes the Canadian passenger liner "Princess Marguerite" on the liner's daily summer trip between Seattle and Victoria, B.C. The snow-crested Olympics mark the distant horizon.

(Lower Right) LA CONNER ... La Conner is a historic and still-busy village on the shore of Puget Sound. It is a port for San Juan Island fishing boats and lies on the western edge of the Skagit Valley agriculture area.

(Upper Left) GREEN RIVER GORGE ... The cool depths of beautiful Green River Gorge in Puget Sound is a popular rendezvous for swimmers and picnickers in summer months.

(Upper Right) SAN JUAN ISLANDS ... Roche Harbor is probably the most popular rendezvous for pleasure boaters in the San Juan Islands. The harbor is protected from weather by several little islands and jutting peninsulas.
(Lower) DECEPTION PASS STATE PARK ... Pleasure boaters enjoy the challenge and thrills of bucking turbulent tidal currents that rush through the narrow channels between Fidalgo and Whidby islands, on the eastern edge of the San Juan Islands. Deception Pass State Park is one of the most exciting and popular parks in the Northwest.
(Upper Left) LA PUSH ... Offshore islands and rocks provide a background for the fishing boat harbor of La Push. Indians of the Quillayute Reservation head out to sea from their protected port.

(Lower) PORT MADISON ... A snug little harbor at Port Madison on Bainbridge Island in Puget Sound, Washington, is used by the Seattle Yacht Club as well as by other boaters and commercial fishermen who have homes around the shoreline of the cove. Historic Port Madison is only a short trip by private boat or ferry from Seattle.

(Upper) PORT MADISON ... The land-locked harbor of Port Madison is a favorite rendezvous for pleasure and fishing boats. It is also a choice setting for home sites. The natural advantages of this beautiful cove were put to practical use in the 1850s when historic Fort Madison was located here.

(Upper) PUGET SOUND SUNSET ... The setting sun blazes a golden path across the waters of Puget Sound framed by timber along the famed Chuckanut Drive in northern Washington.
(Lower) SAN JUAN ISLANDS ... A tranquil farm scene on an Orcas Island cove. Orcas island is one of the 172 islands which comprise the famed San Juan Group in Puget Sound.

(Left) MT. ADAMS ... A logging road curves through autumn foliage in Gifford Pinchot National Forest at the foot of Mt. Adams.
(Upper Left) GLACIER PEAK WILDERNESS ... This trail is one of two which climb into the heart of the Glacier Peak Wilderness through miles of virgin evergreen forests of the Suiattle River Valley.
(Upper Right) NORTH CASCADES HIGHWAY ... Open alpine slopes reach up to an impressive peak overlooking the North Cascades Highway.
(Lower) NORTH CASCADES NATIONAL PARK ... Magic Mountain and other glacier-clad peaks are viewed from meadows of Sahale Arm.

(Upper Right) BUCK CREEK ... The clear cold waters of Buck Creek hurry down a North Cascades slope, splashing over a bed of colorful granite boulders beside giant evergreen trees.

(Upper Left) GLACIER PEAK WILDERNESS ... An old snag on Miners Ridge high above Image Lake creates a dramatic foreground for this photo of Glacier Peak. This is the heart of the vast Glacier Peak Wilderness, which can be visited only by trail.

(Lower) WASHINGTON CASCADES ... Cathedral Rock towers several thousand feet above Fish Lake in the Central Cascade Range.

The Mountains

THE CASCADES are the mountainous barrier dividing the "wet" side from the "dry" side of Washington. The fir forests of western Washington are jungle-like, especially on the Olympic Peninsula; the eastern forests are much more open, sparse woods, mostly pine. As a unified range the Cascades are probably unequalled in this country. The Washington Cascades have an additional distinction in that their northern segment contains generally higher and more jagged peaks than the rest of the range. The Washington Cascades are also more glaciated than any other range in the United States. Not as high as the Rockies, the Cascades are more spectacular. The Rockies stand on a mile-and-a-half-high plateau; the Cascades have their bases near sea level and rise uninterrupted 6,000 to 9,000 feet. Volcanic peaks in the range—like Mt. Baker, Glacier Peak, Mt. Rainier, Mt. Adams, and Mt. St. Helens—tower above the rest of the range. The tallest and most massive is 14,410-foot Mt. Rainier, biggest in the contiguous 48 states. A few mountains are officially taller, but they are high points on ridges. Mt. Rainier stands alone, twice as high as peaks around it.

Mt. Rainier's glaciers also set it apart. Its 26 active glaciers comprise the largest single-peak system in the continental United States. The enormous mountain can be seen for great distances north-south and east-west when the weather is right, so it is really a landmark and check point for all of Washington, and neighboring areas as well. It has been set aside as a national park and contains virgin timber whose like may never be seen again. Its slopes are carpeted with wildflowers when the snow melts, and the roads of its park cross four plant zones. Rainier creates its own weather, and with Puget Sound only 40 miles away, the interaction of the mountain's cold bulk with the moist winds from the west makes for some formidable weather. The summer months offer the best weather for exploring the mountain's various landscapes. The snow on the trails at 6,000 feet (Paradise Valley level) is usually gone by mid-July. Within the park are roads from which the mountain can be seen in its many different aspects, in addition to campgrounds, and good hiking trails from which to take closeup looks at the wilderness. There's even a guide service that takes climbing parties to Rainier's very summit, in a two-day trip.

Mt. Adams and Mt. St. Helens, to the south, have been discussed in the chapter on southern Washington. The North Cascades are left for us to define and to study. Up to very recently, no road crossed these wide and rugged peaks. Now the North Cascades Highway breaches the mountains from Diablo Dam on the west and the Methow Valley on the east.

The Cascades Range is about 50 miles wide through Washington, except in the northern mountains, which are about twice that width. Glacier Peak, Mt. Baker, and Mt. Shuksan are the dominant spires. Until the new highway was finished, all roads into this area were old logging or mining roads. Glacier Peak Wilderness itself is open only by trail. (see picture, page 63) Many roads on the west and south sides of the wilderness lead to low-level camping areas from which streamside trails can be followed up into the high country.

The new road across the North Cascades is the culmination of a 100-year-old dream. Fur trader Alexander Ross wrote in his diary, in 1814, of exploring these mountains. A few men like Ross, traders and trappers, were for years the only humans to venture into the rugged land. The California gold strike of 1849 excited prospectors to move northward and begin working streams through Oregon and Washington. Ruby-colored stones, found with the gold nuggets that started the rush into the North Cascades in 1858, gave Ruby Creek its name. The creek flows along the west side of the present highway (State 20), emptying into Ross Lake. The gold rush lasted only one year in the North Cascades, the primary reason for its brevity being the hardships and difficult access problems posed by this primitive area. Another shortlived flurry of gold fever struck about 20 years later, when gold was found in the headwaters of the Skagit River. This, too, was doomed by lack of transportation. Miners and cattlemen in the Okanogan Valley began around this time to petition the legislature of the new state for help in getting their products to market. In 1893 the legislators appropriated $20,000 to build 200 miles of road from Bellingham Bay to the Columbia River via Ruby Creek—$100 a mile for a road through what is probably the most rugged section of the United States. In 1896 a wagon road was started from Marblemount along the Cascade River. The following year it was impassable because of slides and washouts. The road was extended to near Cascade Pass in the 1930s.

(Preceding Page) NORTH CASCADE RANGE ... Winchester Mountain in Mt. Baker National Forest commands a superlative panorama of the rugged peaks of the North Cascade Range. Included in this view looking over one of Twin Lakes are distant peaks of North Cascade National Park, dominated by Mt. Shuksan. Goat Mountain, in Mt. Baker National Forest, is the most prominent peak in the center foreground. Twin Lakes offers camping and fishing, and serves as base camp for hikers and mountaineers.

THE MOUNTAINS

The North Cross-State Highway Association, a group organized in the 1950s, was primarily responsible for the eventual completion of the cross-mountain road. The final route, begun in 1960, was up Ruby, Granite, and Early Winters creeks.

Some of the breathtaking scenery along the new road includes the Ross Lake National Recreation area and its three lakes—Gorge, Diablo, and Ross—strung out along the highway. These are lakes formed by the Skagit River Hydroelectric Project, furnishing power to the city of Seattle. Diablo Lake is especially beautiful with its blue-green color that results from the fine sediment carried to it by streams coming out of glaciers. Ross Dam, 540 feet high, is the tallest of the three dams in the project.

The "eternal snows" of the Cascades, and especially the North Cascades, are caused by the enormous snow packs—20 feet deep in the higher elevations—accumulated during the season of snowfall. Avalanches sometimes isolate mountain communities here during the winter months. The glaciers and icy spires of these mountains are the remnant of the last ice age 10,000 years ago which created the area's alpine scenery — U-shaped valleys, horns, serrated ridges, hanging valleys, and cirque or tarn lakes. This is really glacier country: of the 1,100 glaciers in the continental United States, Washington has 800.

Even the most fearsomely rugged parts of the earth can be quite fragile. Now that the North Cascades have been opened to relatively easy access more and more people will be able to motor into that mountain fastness and find rejuvenation of spirit at a relatively low cost in terms of effort. This may not be all to the good. An old axiom that might be applied here observes that whatever is to be truly appreciated is not won without a struggle. But let us assume that we have grown up enough so that the corollary of that axiom need not apply, to wit: what man obtains with ease he is quick to despoil.

———

(Following Two Pages) COOPER LAKE ... The rugged snow-mantled crests of Washington's Cascade Mountains are reflected on the mirror-like waters of Cooper Lake, nestled in evergreen forests far below.

Central Washington

THE "east slope" is the central part of Washington, distinct, like a comparable region of Oregon, from the west and east parts. It runs all the way from the Canadian border to Oregon on the south. With the Cascades on one side and the Columbia River on the other, this central strip has managed very well to be neither beholden to Seattle or Spokane and their spheres. Its cities are thriving centers for the agricultural prosperity of the farmlands and orchards of the central valleys. Yakima, Ellensburg, Wenatchee, Chelan, and Okanogan supply not only Washington but the whole country with fruit and produce. The famous Washington apples are sent all over the world from this area. The dams on the middle Columbia and on the Yakima River have been crucial to the fairly recent agricultural exploitation of this part of the state. The Columbia dams have, in addition, made ports again out of these inland towns. Not only has this been accomplished, but the great amounts of power supplied by the dams have increased the area's industrial potential.

In north central Washington there is no clearly defined boundary where the east slope of the Cascades leaves off. The mountains just go on, never subsiding into plains or valleys, except for the narrow Okanogan Valley, a wild yet hospitable country popular as a summer resort area. This area of the central belt, reaching south to the Columbia and north to the border, is called the Okanogan Highlands. The great river's east-west course in this part of the state ends at Pateros, where the Columbia turns south and is joined by the Methow River, whose pastoral valley leads up into the high northern Cascades.

One of the most remarkable features of north-central Washington is Lake Chelan, a natural lake lying in a glacial trough whose lower end was dammed up long ago by a colossal terminal moraine. The lake is 60 miles long, and the translation of its Indian name is "deep water." A depth of 1,600 feet has been recorded for the lake. A passenger- and mail-carrying launch, "Lady of the Lake," makes a daily trip from Chelan at the lower end to Stehekin 55 miles away at the head of the lake. Visitors can ride all the way or be put ashore at the many isolated campgrounds along the way. In the summer months a Forest Service ranger goes along and describes points of interest to passengers. The town of Stehekin can be reached only by boat, seaplane, or foot trail over the Cascades. It is set amid a sumptuous alpine landscape whose jagged peaks are 8,500 to 9,500 feet high and still relatively anonymous to everyone but those dedicated recreationists who have fought hard to preserve this region in its natural state. The Lake Chelan National Recreation Area was established by Congress with the specific prohibition against the construction of roads from the outside world to the Stehekin Valley.

Wenatchee sits in mid-state between the north-south borders. Its big-money crop is apples. Its apple orchards line up on both sides of the Columbia and a long way up the Wenatchee River valley. The hardy Winesap and Delicious varieties grown here have a special "bite" that makes them great eating apples, and a "build" that insures long-lasting quality. That's why they can be shipped all over the globe. The Wenatchee Apple Blossom Festival has become a traditional celebration as well as a tourist attraction.

Yakima is the largest and still the most booming of the east-slope cities. It may not have as famous a rodeo as Ellensburg, 37 miles north on U.S. 97, but it is the hub of the Yakima valley, an area of immense importance economically, and becoming more so. A good idea of the valley's riches can be obtained by taking a loop trip from Yakima to Prosser along the Yakima River, returning on the other side of the river. Along the way are lush fruit orchards, fields of produce, hop yards, and vineyards, and it is possible to purchase (or even pick) produce right from the field. At Cherry Hill, near Granger, there is a panoramic and detailed view of the lower valley. Yakima celebrates the climax of harvest season with the Central Washington Fair late in September.

Ellensburg's rodeo is a logical reflection of its situation on the plains, where both horses and alfalfa are raised. East of Ellensburg near Vantage, on the Columbia's bank, is the Ginkgo Petrified Forest. It was formed when lava invaded a lake full of watersoaked ginkgo logs. Mineral deposits gradually replaced wood fiber, turning the logs into stone. A museum on the site illustrates how all this happened.

Horse Heaven Hills, between the Yakima Valley and the Columbia River, is a formerly arid region that has become prosperous in recent times because of increased rainfall. It is a rather remote area where wild horses used to roam and some of them still do, it is said. The hills rise higher and higher as they stretch from the river west through the Yakima Indian

CENTRAL WASHINGTON

Reservation toward the Cascades.

The central Washington belt seems an obvious receiving area for the expanding number of people who have lately "discovered" the Northwest. Its mild climate and lush, protected valleys invite settlement. But one hopes it won't come about in so massive a tide that the east slope valleys become congested with people.

(Following Two Pages) MT. SHUKSAN ... Mt. Shuksan, its rugged crags and glaciers covered by a brand-new cloak of snow, touches the clouds above autumn-tinted alpine meadows surrounding Picture Lake in the new North Cascades National Park. The lake and foreground area are not in the park.

Eastern Washington

THE catchy term, "Inland Empire," is used as an omnibus phrase to mean any part of the country within Spokane's sphere of influence. This takes in parts of Idaho, Montana, and Oregon, as well as eastern Washington. Spokane claims all of Washington from the Cascade slope east, but since the central belt has become an economic entity of its own, able to ship directly to its markets (see Central Washington), Spokane's dominion has diminished somewhat so far as Washington is concerned.

The *real* eastern side of Washington, roughly the dividing line where the Columbia River winds through the state, is in night-and-day contrast to the "wet half" west of the Cascades. The central belt has this difference too, but in a milder way. The Columbia Basin lands between that river and the Snake in the southeast would be close to pure desert were it not for the gigantic system of dams on these two rivers in Washington. The eastern lands used to be typical "Wild West," with endless stretches of dry, open spaces, cattle ranges, and wheat fields, with considerable mining activity in the mountains to the north. But Grand Coulee and the lesser Basin projects have changed all that, if not in substance at least in emphasis. Agriculture is now about as varied as anywhere in the country, and many of the tiny villages in these parts have grown up into good-sized cities.

Spokane, as the hub of its "empire," has benefited most from the various irrigation and hydroelectric projects. It has become the second city in Washington and, as an expression of its new eminence, mounted an extraordinarily successful world's fair—Expo 74—in 1974. But Spokane's growth has escaped much of the uglification that seems to be an adjunct of city growth. The beautiful and turbulent Spokane River, which cuts through the city (and Expo 74), is kept as nearly as possible the way nature made it, both in and outside of the city (see picture, page 47). At 5,514-acre Riverside State Park near the city, the river rushes through a lava gorge shaded by pines. Within a 50-mile radius of Spokane are 76 lakes, most with gently sloping beaches and some thrusting watery fingers back into the hills.

Mt. Spokane, 34 miles northeast, is in the center of a 24,000-acre state park, Washington's largest. The mountain, 5,800 feet high, is a popular skiing area and from its summit can be seen mountains and lakes in Washington, Idaho, and Montana. Fishing and hunting are excellent in this area, and game animals include deer, elk, and even bear. Although Spokane has been tamed since the days when it was the whoop-it-up place for miners, ranchers, and construction workers, it hasn't lost the color and individuality of its beginnings in its rise to big-city status.

The Columbia Basin includes just about all of eastern Washington except the mountainous regions in the north. Uncounted millions of years ago, over a period of many centuries, molten rock poured over a volcanic landscape in central and eastern Washington. Then glaciers came, melted, and wore coulees, or canyons, in the volcanic layers. The biggest hollow was Grand Coulee. The waters from the last ice age created a giant river that was the forerunner of the present-day Columbia River. In volume it would make today's great river seem insignificant by comparison. When the glacial torrent receded and the Columbia settled into its bed, vast areas of the rich, volcanic soil were left dry. Until the Columbia Basin Reclamation Project was completed, the potential of the region for supporting human populations was untapped. The monumental dam that is the key to Basin irrigation, Grand Coulee Dam, is shown in day and night photos on page 45. It is 550 feet high and 4,173 feet long. Canals and reservoirs carry its impounded waters far and wide.

The lake created by this colossal dam is a colossal lake, stretching 150 miles from the dam to the Canadian border. Its 660 miles of shoreline are included within the Coulee Dam National Recreation Area. From the north end of Roosevelt Lake a scenic trip can be made, encompassing a river valley called the Sanpoil whose gentle aspect is a startling contrast to the Roosevelt Lake area and coulee country. The valley can be reached by the Sherman Creek road (State 30) west from Kettle Falls, and by crossing Sherman Pass, the highest in Washington. From the pass there are views of Roosevelt Lake on the east and south, and the Okanogan Highlands and Cascades to the west. State Highway 21 is taken heading south from the town of Republic, following the narrow river valley, with its pine forests and farmlands.

The coulee country is in the heart of eastern Washington. It is a region of geological wonders—old lava flows, dry river beds, and fossil caves. Dry Falls State Park, south of Grand Coulee, provides an illustration. Dry Falls is believed to have been one of the greatest

EASTERN WASHINGTON

falls ever formed. From a vantage point in the park can be seen the five huge recesses or alcoves over which the water flowed, dropping 400 feet over an extent of 3½ miles. The desert country below Dry Falls has natural lakes that occur in a 20-mile stretch of the lower coulee and help make the area one of eastern Washington's most popular vacation spots. It's a land full of strange formations, odd rocks, and other things that make life pleasant for geologists.

Irrigation has spread south from Coulee Dam and created farmlands out of what was once millions of acres of desert. In the many coulees that cut into these plains can be seen millions of years of geologic time. Inspection of these layers is especially easy to do by car on State Highway 155, which follows Grand Coulee.

At the town of Moses Lake, a bit to the south, is a splendid museum which describes and illustrates with specimens the history and geology of the region. Just a little farther to the south is Potholes Reservoir, created by O'Sullivan Dam, and filling a whole valley with its vast waters.

The southeast corner of Washington is a land of bleak vistas, deep chasms, and arid mountains, a stretch of end-of-the-world landscape whose character is emphasized by the deep gorge of Hell's Canyon to the east, and the swift-flowing Snake River rushing through it. The Blue Mountains dominate the region that borders Oregon, spreading across the line into that state. Service roads are the only ones that penetrate the lonely fastnesses of the Blue Mountains, although there is a 263-mile highway loop around them, including the Oregon segment. A dirt road that crosses these mountains from Dayton to Tollgate, Oregon, is driveable only in summer. From Asotin, near the Idaho border, a dirt road follows the Snake for a while, but turns away toward the Grande Ronde where that river comes up from Oregon. The north leg of U.S. Highway 12, from Walla Walla to Clarkston, roughly follows the route of the Snake, skirting the Blue Mountains and passing through some peaceful little towns that used to be swingers when they were on the stagecoach route and entertained miners and gamblers. Lewis and Clark passed this way, and some of the places along the road claim honors as places where the celebrated explorers stopped over, including Lewis and Clark Trail State Park between Waitsburg and Dayton.

Walla Walla (an Indian name meaning "many waters") began as a boom town. It was a base for gold prospectors on their way to Idaho in the 1860s. Nowadays it is an agricultural center with a big canning industry, growing primarily wheat and peas. Whitman College, the oldest in the state, is at Walla Walla. The Whitman Mission, established in 1836, is nearby. It was a haven for migrants traveling over the Oregon Trail in the earlier days of the westward movement. Traffic into Washington ceased around mid-century as wagon trains began heading more directly to the Willamette Valley in Oregon. The Whitmans and others of the mission were massacred by the Indians in the wars of the fifties.

The Indian wars broke out in earnest after a peace treaty had been signed in 1855. Colonel Steptoe and some troops from Walla Walla had marched north to the area of a butte 30 miles south of a trading post later to become Spokane. The Indians, encamped on the butte, had visual command of the whole Palouse country and saw him coming. The colonel and his men were soundly thrashed. Oddly, the infamous butte was later named for the colonel. Steptoe Butte, near the town of Rosalia, rises 3,600 feet above the plateau. It is an ancient mountain whose top was untouched by the lava flows that spread over the Columbia Basin after the mountain had formed. Steptoe, by the way, fared better than Custer did some years later. He and his men were surrounded on a hill but managed to slip across the Snake River at night when the overconfident Indians relaxed their guard, intending to finish off the troops the next day.

For a time the Snake was considered by both sides as the boundary line for settlers, but when gold was found in Idaho, hordes of whites poured in by land and by river. Steamboats charged up the Snake to Lewiston, then up the Clearwater River. In later days the Snake was the prime route for transporting wheat, which was lowered by tramway over cliffs some 2,000 feet high to barges in the canyons northeast of Pomeroy.

The Palouse River cuts an impressive figure through this country. On the way to its junction with the Snake it has carved a deep canyon of its own, one feature of which is Palouse Falls, dropping 198 feet into the canyon.

The "other-world" contrasts that are scattered through much of eastern Washington may impart a

(Upper Right) ROSS LAKE NATIONAL RECREATION AREA ... Power dams on the Skagit River in the North Cascade Range have created three lakes which are now in the Ross Lake National Recreation Area. This is Diablo Lake, its waters tinted by dissolved glacial silt.

(Upper Left) SAUK MOUNTAIN ... A growth of evergreens clings defiantly to the wind-swept crest of the Sauk Mountain in the North Cascade Range.

(Lower) AMERICAN RIVER ... The American River rushes down the slopes of the Cascades. Cottonwood and evergreen trees border the stream in this autumn scene.

valuable lesson to us by reason of their strangeness, a lesson on the capacity of nature for infinite variety. In the natural realm, all things can be and often are replaced, and in their stead arises a new creation sometimes vastly different from and superior to the one that had existed. We may well ponder the evidence.

Washington

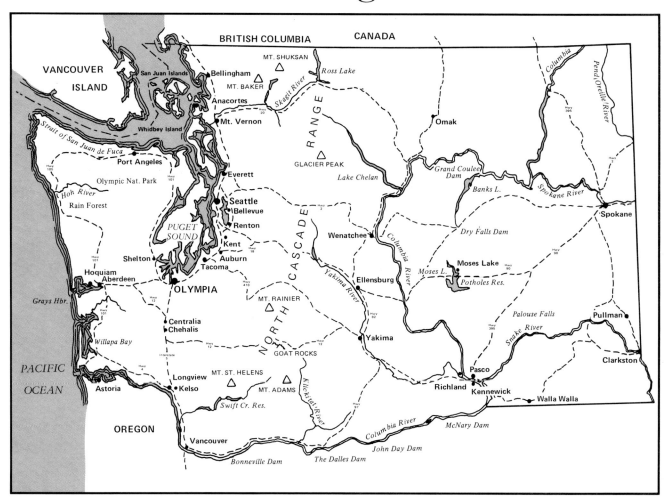

Wildflowers of Washington

TRILLIUM

Harbinger of spring is the trillium blossom. The trillium is one of the first plants to bloom in the new season. As the flower ages, it gradually changes from white to deep purple.

WILD RHODODENDRON

A colorful bloom and buds of wild rhododendron are displayed here. These showy wild shrubs flourish in western Oregon, western Washington and northwestern California. It is the Washington state flower.

TIGER LILY   (Lilium columbiaum)

It grows in various areas of the Northwest.

WILD CURRANT

Wild currant blooms profusely in western valleys and foothills of the Pacific Northwest. This beautiful flowering shrub is one of the earliest of the wildflowers in the Northwest.

MOUNT RAINIER NATIONAL PARK

Wild flowers bloom in profusion in the high alpine meadows of Mount Rainier National Park.

PINK MIMULUS   (Mimulus Lewisii)

Blooms of Mimulus add color beside a small stream in North Cascades National Park.

(Preceding Page) WASHINGTON COAST ... The Cape Disappointment Lighthouse stands guard as an ocean freighter heads out to sea from the mouth of the Columbia River.

MT. RAINIER NATIONAL PARK

WILD RHODODENDRON

TIGER LILY

WILD CURRANT

TRILLIUM

PINK MIMULUS